On Old Age

Cicero

Table of Contents

On Old Age.

Cicero

```
  And should my service, Titus, ease the weight
Of care that wrings your heart, and draw the sting
Which rankles there, what guerdon shall there be?
```

On Old Age

FOR I may address you, Atticus, in the lines in which Flamininus was addressed by the man who, poor in wealth, was rich in honour's gold, though I am well assured that you are not, as Flamininus was, kept on the rack of care by night and day.

For I know how well—ordered and equable your mind is, and am fully aware that it was not a surname alone which you brought home with you from Athens, but its culture and good sense. And yet I have an idea that you are at times stirred to the heart by the same circumstances as myself. To console you for these is a more serious matter, and must be put off to another time. For the present I have resolved to dedicate to you an essay on Old Age. For from the burden of impending or at least advancing age, common to us both, I would do something to relieve us both: though as to yourself I am fully aware that you support and will support it, as you do everything else, with calmness and philosophy. But directly I resolved to write on old age, you at once occurred to me as deserving a gift of which both of us might take advantage. To myself, indeed, the composition of this book has been so delightful that it has not only wiped away all the disagreeables of old age, but has even made it luxurious and delightful too. Never, therefore, can philosophy be praised as highly as it deserves, considering that its faithful disciple is able to spend every period of his life with unruffled feelings. However, on other subjects I have spoken at large, and shall often speak again: this book which I herewith send you is on Old Age. I have put the whole discourse not, as Alisto of Cos did, in the mouth of Tithonus—for a mere fable would have lacked conviction—but in that of Marcus Cato when he was an old man, to give my essay greater weight. I represent Lælius and Scipio at his house expressing surprise at his carrying his years so lightly, and Cato answering them. If he shall seem to shew somewhat more learning in this discourse than he generally did in his own books, put it down to the Greek literature of which it is known that he became an eager student in his old age. But what need of more? Cato's own words will at once explain all I feel about old age.

```
        M. CATO.
PUBLIUS CORNELIUS SCIPIO AFRICANUS (the younger).
        GAIUS LAELIUS.
```

On Old Age

Scipio. Many a time have I in conversation with my friend Gaius Lælius here expressed my admiration, Marcus Cato, of the eminent, nay perfect, wisdom displayed by you indeed at all points, but above everything because I have noticed that old age never seemed a burden to you, while to most old men it is so hateful that they declare themselves under a weight heavier than Aetna.

Cato. Your admiration is easily excited, it seems, my dear Scipio and Lælius. Men, of course, who have no resources in themselves for securing a good and happy life find every age burdensome. But those who look for all happiness from within can never think anything bad which Nature makes inevitable. In that category before anything else comes old age, to which all wish to attain, and at which all grumble when attained. Such is Folly's inconsistency and unreasonableness! They say that it is stealing upon them faster than they expected. In the first place, who compelled them to hug an illusion? For in what respect did old age steal upon manhood faster than manhood upon childhood? In the next place, in what way would old age have been less disagreeable to them if they were in their eight–hundredth year than in their eightieth? For their past, however long, when once it was past, would have no consolation for a stupid old age. Wherefore, if it is your wont to admire my wisdom—and I would that it were worthy of your good opinion and of my own surname of Sapiens—it really consists in the fact that I follow Nature, the best of guides, as I would a god, and am loyal to her commands. It is not likely, if she has written the rest of the play well, that she has been careless about the last act like some idle poet. But after all some "last" was inevitable, just as to the berries of a tree and the fruits of the earth there comes in the fulness of time a period of decay and fall. A wise man will not make a grievance of this. To rebel against Nature—is not that to fight like the giants with the gods?

Lælius. And yet, Cato, you will do us a very great favour (I venture to speak for Scipio as for myself) if—since we all hope, or at least wish, to become old men—you would allow us to learn from you in good time before it arrives, by what methods we may most easily acquire the strength to support the burden of advancing age.

Cato. I will do so without doubt, Lælius, especially if, as you say, it will be agreeable to you both.

Lælius. We do wish very much, Cato, if it is no trouble to you, to be allowed to see the nature of the bourne which you have reached after completing a long journey, as it were, upon which we too are bound to embark.

Cato. I will do the best I can, Lælius. It has often been my fortune to hear the complaints of my contemporaries—like will to like, you know, according to the old proverb—complaints to which men like C. Salinator and Sp. Albinus, who were of consular rank and about my time, used to give vent. They were, first, that they had lost the pleasures of the senses, without which they did not regard life as life at all; and, secondly, that they were neglected by those from whom they had been used to receive attentions. Such men appear to me to lay the blame on the wrong thing. For if it had been the fault of old age, then these same misfortunes would have befallen me and all other men of advanced years. But I have known many of them who never said a word of complaint against old age; for they were only too glad to be freed from the bondage of passion, and were not at all looked down upon by their friends. The fact is that the blame for all complaints of that kind is to be charged to character, not to a particular time of life. For old men who are reasonable and neither cross-grained nor churlish find old age tolerable enough: whereas unreason and churlishness cause uneasiness at every time of life.

Lælius. It is as you say, Cato. But perhaps some one may suggest that it is your large means, wealth, and high position that make you think old age tolerable: whereas such good fortune only falls to few.

Cato. There is something in that, Lælius, but by no means all. For instance, the story is told of the answer of Themistocles in a wrangle with a certain Seriphian, who asserted that he owed his brilliant position to the reputation of his country, not to his own. "If I had been a Seriphian," said he, "even I should never have been famous, nor would you if you had been an Athenian." Something like this may be said of old age. For the philosopher himself could not find old age easy to bear in the depths of poverty, nor the fool feel it anything but a burden though he were a millionaire. You may be sure, my dear Scipio and Lælius, that the arms best adapted to old age are culture and the active exercise of the virtues. For if they have been maintained at every period—if one has lived much as well as long—the harvest they produce is wonderful, not only because they never fail us even in our last days (though that in itself is supremely important), but also because the consciousness of a well-spent life and the recollection of many virtuous actions are exceedingly delightful.

4

On Old Age

Take the case of Q. Fabius Maximus, the man, I mean, who recovered Tarentum. When I was a young man and he an old one, I was as much attached to him as if he had been my contemporary. For that great man's serious dignity was tempered by courteous manners, nor had old age made any change in his character. True, he was not exactly an old man when my devotion to him began, yet he was nevertheless well on in life; for his first consulship fell in the year after my birth. When quite a stripling I went with him in his fourth consulship as a soldier in the ranks, on the expedition against Capua, and in the fifth year after that against Tarentum. Four years after that I was elected quæstor, holding office in the consulship of Tuditanus and Cethegus, in which year, indeed, he as a very old man spoke in favour of the Cincian law "on gifts and fees."

Now this man conducted wars with all the spirit of youth when he was far advanced in life, and by his persistence gradually wearied out Hannibal, when rioting in all the confidence of youth. How brilliant are those lines of my friend Ennius on him!

For us, down beaten by the storms of fate,

One man by wise delays restored the State.

Praise or dispraise moved not his constant mood,

True to his purpose, to his country's good!

Down ever–lengthening avenues of fame

Thus shines and shall shine still his glorious name.

Again, what vigilance, what profound skill did he shew in the capture of Tarentum! It was indeed in my hearing that he made the famous retort to Salinator, who had retreated into the citadel after losing the town: "It was owing to me, Quintus Fabius, that you retook Tarentum." "Quite so," he replied with a laugh; "for had you not lost it, I should never have recovered it." Nor was he less eminent in civil life than in war. In his second consulship, though his colleague would not move in the matter, he resisted as long as he could the proposal of the tribune C. Flaminius to divide the territory of the Picenians and Gauls in free allotments in defiance of a resolution of the Senate. Again, though he was an augur, he ventured to say that whatever was done in the interests of the State was done with the best possible auspices, that any laws proposed against its interest were proposed against the auspices. I was cognisant of much that was admirable in that great man, but nothing struck me with greater astonishment than the way in which he bore the death of his son—a man of brilliant character and who had been consul. His funeral speech over him is in wide circulation, and when we read it, is there any philosopher of whom we do not think meanly? Nor in truth was he only great in the light of day and in the sight of his fellow–citizens; he was still more eminent in private and at home. What a wealth of conversation! What weighty maxims! What a wide acquaintance with ancient history! What an accurate knowledge of the science of augury! For a Roman, too, he had a great tincture of letters. He had a tenacious memory for military history of every sort, whether of Roman or foreign wars. And I used at that time to enjoy his conversation with a passionate eagerness, as though I already divined, what actually turned out to be the case, that when he died there would be no one to teach me anything.

What then is the purpose of such a long disquisition on Maximus? It is because you now see that an old age like his cannot conscientiously be called unhappy. Yet it is after all true that everybody cannot be a Scipio or a Maximus, with stormings of cities, with battles by land and sea, with wars in which they themselves commanded, and with triumphs to recall. Besides this there is a quiet, pure, and cultivated life which produces a calm and gentle old age, such as we have been told Plato's was, who died at his writing–desk in his eighty–first year; or like that of Isocrates, who says that he wrote the book called The Panegyric in his ninety–fourth year, and who lived for five years afterwards; while his master Gorgias of Leontini completed a hundred and seven years without ever relaxing his diligence or giving up work. When some one asked him why he consented to remain so long alive—"I have no fault," said he, "to find with old age." That was a noble answer, and worthy of a scholar. For fools impute their own frailties and guilt to old age, contrary to the practice of Ennius, whom I mentioned just now. In the lines—

Like some brave steed that oft before

The Olympic wreath of victory bore,

Now by the weight of years oppressed,

Forgets the race, and takes his rest—

he compares his own old age to that of a high–spirited and successful race–horse. And him indeed you may very well remember. For the present consuls Titus Flamininus and Manius Acilius were elected in the nineteenth year after his death; and his death occurred in the consulship of Capeio and Philippus, the latter consul for the second time: in which year I, then sixty–six–years old, spoke in favour of the Voconian law in a voice that was still strong and with lungs still sound; while he, though seventy years old, supported two burdens considered the heaviest of all—poverty and old age—in such a way as to be all but fond of them.

The fact is that when I come to think it over, I find that there are four reasons for old age being thought unhappy: First, that it withdraws us from active employments; second, that it enfeebles the body; third, that it deprives us of nearly all physical pleasures; fourth, that it is the next step to death. Of each of these reasons, if you will allow me, let us examine the force and justice separately.

OLD AGE WITHDRAWS US FROM ACTIVE EMPLOYMENTS. From which of them? Do you mean from those carried on by youth and bodily strength? Are there then no old men's employments to be after all conducted by the intellect, even when bodies are weak? So then Q. Maximus did nothing; nor L. Aemilius—your father, Scipio, and my excellent son's father–in–law! So with other old men—the Fabricii, the Curii and Coruncanii—when they were supporting the State by their advice and influence, they were doing nothing! To old age Appius Claudius had the additional disadvantage of being blind; yet it was he who, when the Senate was inclining towards a peace with Pyrrhus and was for making a treaty, did not hesitate to say what Ennius has embalmed in the verses:

Whither have swerved the souls so firm of yore?

Is sense grown senseless? Can feet stand no more?

And so on in a tone of the most passionate vehemence. You know the poem, and the speech of Appius himself is extant. Now, he delivered it seventeen years after his second consulship, there having been an interval of ten years between the two consulships, and he having been censor before his previous consulship. This will show you that at the time of the war with Pyrrhus he was a very old man. Yet this is the story handed down to us.

On Old Age

There is therefore nothing in the arguments of those who say that old age takes no part in public business. They are like men who would say that a steersman does nothing in sailing a ship, because, while some of the crew are climbing the masts, others hurrying up and down the gangways, others pumping out the bilge water, he sits quietly in the stern holding the tiller. He does not do what young men do; nevertheless he does what is much more important and better. The great affairs of life are not performed by physical strength, or activity, or nimbleness of body, but by deliberation, character, expression of opinion. Of these old age is not only not deprived, but, as a rule, has them in a greater degree. Unless by any chance I, who as a soldier in the ranks, as military tribune, as legate, and as consul have been employed in various kinds of war, now appear to you to be idle because not actively engaged in war. But I enjoin upon the Senate what is to be done, and how. Carthage has long been harbouring evil designs, and I accordingly proclaim war against her in good time. I shall never cease to entertain fears about her till I hear of her having been levelled with the ground. The glory of doing that I pray that the immortal gods may reserve for you, Scipio, so that you may complete the task begun by your grandfather, now dead more than thirty-two years ago; though all years to come will keep that great man's memory green. He died in the year before my censorship, nine years after my consulship, having been returned consul for the second time in my own consulship. If then he had lived to his hundredth year, would he have regretted having lived to be old? For he would of course not have been practising rapid marches, nor dashing on a foe, nor hurling spears from a distance, nor using swords at close quarters—but only counsel, reason, and senatorial eloquence. And if those qualities had not resided in us seniors, our ancestors would never have called their supreme council a Senate. At Sparta, indeed, those who hold the highest magistracies are in accordance with the fact actually called "elders." But if you will take the trouble to read or listen to foreign history, you will find that the mightiest States have been brought into peril by young men, have been supported and restored by old. The question occurs in the poet Nævius' Sport:

Pray, who are those who brought your State

With such despatch to meet its fate?

There is a long answer, but this is the chief point:

A crop of brand-new orators we grew,

On Old Age

And foolish, paltry lads who thought they knew.

For of course rashness is the note of youth, prudence of old age.

But, it is said, memory dwindles. No doubt, unless you keep it in practice, or if you happen to be somewhat dull by nature. Themistocles had the names of all his fellow–citizens by heart. Do you imagine that in his old age he used to address Aristides as Lysimachus? For my part, I know not only the present generation, but their father, also, and their grandfathers. Nor have I any fear of losing my memory by reading tombstones, according to the vulgar superstition. On the contrary, by reading them I renew my memory of those who are dead and gone. Nor, in point of fact, have I ever heard of any old man forgetting where he had hidden his money. They remember everything that interests them: when to answer to their bail, business appointments, who owes them money, and to whom they owe it. What about lawyers, pontiffs, augurs, philosophers, when old? What a multitude of things they remember! Old men retain their intellects well enough, if only they keep their minds active and fully employed. Nor is that the case only with men of high position and great office: it applies equally to private life and peaceful pursuits. Sophocles composed tragedies to extreme old age; and being believed to neglect the care of his property owing to his devotion to his art, his sons brought him into court to get a judicial decision depriving him of the management of his property on the ground of weak intellect—just as in our law it is customary to deprive a paterfamilias of the management of his property if he is squandering it. Thereupon the old poet is said to have read to the judges the play he had on hand and had just composed—the Oedipus Coloneus—and to have asked them whether they thought that the work of a man of weak intellect. After the reading he was acquitted by the jury. Did old age then compel this man to become silent in his particular art, or Homer, Hesiod, Simonides, or Isocrates and Gorgias, whom I mentioned before, or the founders of schools of philosophy, Pythagoras, Democritus, Plato, Xenocrates, or later Zeno and Cleanthus, or Diogenes the Stoic, whom you too saw at Rome? Is it not rather the case with all these that the active pursuit of study only ended with life?

But, to pass over these sublime studies, I can name some rustic Romans from the Sabine district, neighbours and friends of my own, without whose presence farm work of importance is scarcely ever performed—whether sowing, or harvesting or storing crops. And yet in other things this is less surprising; for no one is so old as to think that he may not live a year. But they bestow their labour on what they know does not affect them in

On Old Age

any case:

He plants his trees to serve a race to come, as our poet Statius says in his Comrades. Nor indeed would a farmer, however old, hesitate to answer any one who asked him for whom he was planting: "For the immortal gods, whose will it was that I should not merely receive these things from my ancestors, but should also hand them on to the next generation."

That remark about the old man is better than the following:

If age brought nothing worse than this,

It were enough to mar our bliss,

That he who bides for many years

Sees much to shun and much for tears.

Yes, and perhaps much that gives him pleasure too. Besides, as to subjects for tears, he often comes upon them in youth as well.

A still more questionable sentiment in the same Cæcilius is:

No greater misery can of age be told

Than this: be sure, the young dislike the old.

Delight in them is nearer the mark than dislike. For just as old men, if they are wise, take pleasure in the society of young men of good parts, and as old age is rendered less dreary for those who are courted and liked by the youth, so also do young men find pleasure in the maxims of the old, by which they are drawn to the pursuit of excellence. Nor do I perceive that you find my society less pleasant than I do yours. But this is enough to show you how, so far from being listless and sluggish, old age is even a busy time, always doing and attempting something, of course of the same nature as each man's taste had been in the previous part of his life. Nay, do not some even add to their stock of learning? We see Solon, for instance, boasting in his poems that he grows old "daily learning something new." Or again in my own case, it was only when an old man that I became acquainted with Greek literature, which in fact I absorbed with such avidity—in my yearning to quench, as it were, a long-continued thirst—that I became acquainted with the very facts which you see me now using as precedents. When I heard what Socrates had done about the lyre I should have liked for my part to have done that too, for the ancients used to learn the lyre, but, at any rate, I worked hard at literature.

Nor, again, do I now MISS THE BODILY STRENGTH OF A YOUNG MAN (for that was the second point as to the disadvantages of old age) any more than as a young man I missed the strength of a bull or an elephant. You should use what you have, and whatever you may chance to be doing, do it with all your might. What could be weaker than Milo of Croton's exclamation? When in his old age he was watching some athletes practising in the course, he is said to have looked at his arms and to have exclaimed with tears in his eyes: "Ah, well! these are now as good as dead." Not a bit more so than yourself, you trifler! For at no time were you made famous by your real self, but by chest and biceps. Sext. Aelius never gave vent to such a remark, nor, many years before him, Titus Coruncanius, nor, more recently, P. Crassus—all of them learned jurisconsults in active practice, whose knowledge of their profession was maintained to their last breath. I am afraid an orator does lose vigour by old age, for his art is not a matter of the intellect alone, but of lungs and bodily strength. Though as a rule that musical ring in the voice even gains in brilliance in a certain way as one grows old—certainly I have not yet lost it, and you see my years. Yet after all the style of speech suitable to an old man is the quiet and unemotional, and it often happens that the chastened and calm delivery of an old man eloquent secures a hearing. If you cannot attain to that yourself, you might still instruct a Scipio and a Lælius. For what is more charming than old age surrounded by the enthusiasm of youth? Shall we not allow old age even the strength to teach the young, to train and equip them for all the duties of life? And what can be a nobler employment? For my part, I used to think Publius and Gnæus Scipio and your two grandfathers, L. Aemilius and P. Africanus, fortunate men when I saw them with a company of young nobles about them. Nor should we think any teachers of the fine arts otherwise than happy, however much their bodily forces may have decayed and failed. And yet that same failure of the bodily forces is more often brought about by the vices of youth than of old age; for a dissolute and intemperate youth hands down the body to old age in a worn-out state. Xenophon's Cyrus, for instance, in his discourse delivered on his death-bed and at a very advanced age, says that he never perceived his old age to have become weaker than his youth had been. I remember as a boy Lucius Metellus, who, having been created Pontifex Maximus four years after his second consulship, held that office twenty–two years, enjoying such excellent strength of body in the very last hours of his life as not to miss his youth. I need not speak of myself; though that indeed is an old man's way and is generally allowed to my time of life. Don't you see in Homer how frequently Nestor talks of his own good qualities? For he was living through a third generation; nor had he any reason to fear that upon saying what was true about himself he should appear either over vain or talkative. For, as Homer says, "from his lips flowed discourse sweeter than honey," for which sweet breath he wanted no bodily strength. And yet, after all, the famous leader of the Greeks nowhere wishes to have ten men like Ajax, but like Nestor: if he could get them, he feels no doubt of Troy shortly falling.

But to return to my own case: I am in my eighty–fourth year. I could wish that I had been able to make the same boast as Cyrus; but, after all, I can say this: I am not indeed as vigorous as I was as a private soldier in the Punic war, or as quæstor in the same war, or as consul in Spain, and four years later when as a military tribune I took part in the engagement at Thermopylæ under the consul Manius Acilius Glabrio; but yet, as you see, old age has not entirely destroyed my muscles, has not quite brought me to the ground. The Senate–house does not find all my vigour gone, nor the rostra, nor my friends, nor my clients, nor my foreign guests. For I have never given in to that ancient and much–praised proverb:

Old when young

Is old for long.

For myself, I had rather be an old man a somewhat shorter time than an old man before my time. Accordingly, no one up to the present has wished to see me, to whom I have been denied as engaged. But, it may be said, I have less strength than either of you. Neither have you the strength of the centurion T. Pontius: is he the more eminent man on that account? Let there be only a proper husbanding of strength, and let each man proportion his efforts to his powers. Such an one will assuredly not be possessed with any great regret for his loss of strength. At Olympia Milo is said to have stepped into the course carrying a live ox on his shoulders. Which then of the two would you prefer to have given to you—bodily strength like that, or intellectual strength like that of Pythagoras? In fine, enjoy that blessing when you have it; when it is gone, don't wish it back—unless we are to think that young men should wish their childhood back, and those somewhat older their youth! The course of life is fixed, and nature admits of its being run but in one way, and only once; and to each part of our life there is something specially seasonable; so that the feebleness of children, as well as the high spirit of youth, the soberness of maturer years, and the ripe wisdom of old age—all have a certain natural advantage which should be secured in its proper season. I think you are informed, Scipio, what your grandfather's foreign friend Masinissa does to this day, though ninety years old. When he has once begun a journey on foot he does not mount his horse at all; when on horseback he never gets off his horse. By no rain or cold can he be induced to cover his head. His body is absolutely free from unhealthy humours, and so he still performs all the duties and functions of a king. Active exercise, therefore, and temperance can preserve some part of one's former strength even in old age.

Bodily strength is wanting to old age; but neither is bodily strength demanded from old men. Therefore, both by law and custom, men of my time of life are exempt from those duties which cannot be supported without bodily strength. Accordingly not only are we not forced to do what we cannot do; we are not even obliged to do as much as we can. But, it will be said, many old men are so feeble that they cannot perform any duty in life of any sort or kind. That is not a weakness to be set down as peculiar to old age: it is one shared by ill health. How feeble was the son of P. Africanus, who adopted you! What weak health he had, or rather no health at all! If that had not been the case, we should have had in him a second brilliant light in the political horizon; for he had added a wider cultivation to his father's greatness of spirit. What wonder then, that old men are eventually feeble, when even young men cannot escape it? My dear Lælius and Scipio, we must stand up against old age and make up for its drawbacks by taking pains. We must fight it as we should an illness. We must look after our health, use moderate exercise, take just enough food and drink to recruit, but not to overload, our strength. Nor is it the body alone that must be supported, but the intellect and soul much more. For they are like lamps: unless you feed them with oil, they too go out from old age. Again, the body is apt to get gross from exercise; but the intellect becomes nimbler by exercising itself. For what Cæcilius means by "old dotards of the comic stage" are the credulous, the forgetful, and the slipshod. These are faults that do not attach to old age as such, but to a sluggish, spiritless, and sleepy old age. Young men are more frequently wanton and dissolute than old men; but yet, as it is not all young men that are so, but the bad set among them, even so senile folly—usually called imbecility—applies to old men of unsound character, not to all. Appius governed four sturdy sons, five daughters, that great establishment, and all those clients, though he was both old and blind. For he kept his mind at full stretch like a bow, and never gave in to old age by growing slack. He maintained not merely an influence but an absolute command over his family: his slaves feared him, his sons were in awe of him, all loved him. In that family, indeed, ancestral custom and discipline were in full vigour. The fact is that old age is respectable just as long as it asserts itself, maintains its proper rights, and is not enslaved to any one. For as I admire a young man who has something of the old man in him, so do I an old one who has something of a young man. The man who aims at this may possibly become old in body—in mind he never will. I am now engaged in composing the seventh book of my Origins. I collect all the records of antiquity. The speeches delivered in all the celebrated cases which I have defended I am at this particular time getting into shape for publication. I am writing treatises on augural, pontifical, and civil law. I am, besides, studying hard at Greek, and after the manner of the Pythagoreans—to keep my memory in working order—I repeat in the evening whatever I have said, heard, or done in the course of each day. These are the exercises of the intellect, these the training–grounds of the mind: while I sweat and labour on these I don't much feel the loss of bodily strength. I appear in court for my friends; I frequently attend the Senate and bring motions before it on my own responsibility, prepared after deep and long reflection. And these I support by my intellectual, not my bodily forces. And if I were not strong enough to do these things, yet I should enjoy my sofa—imagining the very operations which I was now unable to perform. But what makes me capable of doing this is my past life. For a man who is always living in the midst of these studies and labours does not perceive when old age creeps upon him. Thus, by slow and imperceptible degrees life draws to its end. There is no sudden breakage; it just slowly goes out.

The third charge against old age is that it LACKS SENSUAL PLEASURES. What a splendid service does old age render, if it takes from us the greatest blot of youth! Listen, my dear young friends, to a speech of Archytas of Tarentum, among the greatest and most illustrious of men, which was put into my hands when as a young man I was at Tarentum with Q. Maximus. "No ore deadly curse than sensual pleasure has been inflicted on mankind by nature, to gratify which our wanton appetites are roused beyond all prudence or restraint. It is a fruitful source of treasons, revolutions, secret communications with the enemy. In fact, there is no crime, no evil deed, to which the appetite for sensual pleasures does not impel us. Fornications and adulteries, and every abomination of that kind, are brought about by the enticements of pleasure and by them alone. Intellect is the best gift of nature or God: to this divine gift and endowment there is nothing so inimical as pleasure. For when appetite is our master, there is no place for self−control; nor where pleasure reigns supreme can virtue hold its ground. To see this more vividly, imagine a man excited to the highest conceivable pitch of sensual pleasure. It can be doubtful to no one that such a person, so long as he is under the influence of such excitation of the senses, will be unable to use to any purpose either intellect, reason, or thought. Therefore nothing can be so execrable and so fatal as pleasure; since, when more than ordinarily violent and lasting, it darkens all the light of the soul."

These were the words addressed by Archytas to the Samnite Gaius Pontius, father of the man by whom the consuls Spurius Postumius and Titus Veturius were beaten in the battle of Caudium. My friend Nearchus of Tarentum, who had remained loyal to Rome, told me that he had heard them repeated by some old men; and that Plato the Athenian was present, who visited Tarentum, I find, in the consulship of L. Camillus and Appius Claudius.

What is the point of all this? It is to show you that, if we were unable to scorn pleasure by the aid of reason and philosophy, we ought to have been very grateful to old age for depriving us of all inclination for that which it was wrong to do. For pleasure hinders thought, is a foe to reason, and, so to speak, blinds the eyes of the mind. It is, moreover, entirely alien to virtue. I was sorry to have to expel Lucius, brother of the gallant Titus Flamininus, from the Senate seven years after his consulship; but I thought it imperative to affix a stigma on an act of gross sensuality. For when he was in Gaul as consul, he had yielded to the entreaties of his paramour at a dinner−party to behead a man who happened to be in prison condemned on a capital charge. When his brother Titus was Censor, who preceded me, he escaped; but I and Flaccus could not countenance an act of such criminal and abandoned lust, especially as, besides the personal dishonour, it brought disgrace on the Government.

I have often been told by men older than myself, who said that they had heard it as boys from old men, that Gaius Fabricius was in the habit of expressing astonishment at having heard, when envoy at the headquarters of King Pyrrhus, from the Thessalian Cineas, that there was a man of Athens who professed to be a "philosopher," and affirmed that everything we did was to be referred to pleasure. When he told this to Manius Curius and Publius Decius, they used to remark that they wished that the Samnites and Pyrrhus himself would hold the same opinion. It would be much easier to conquer them, if they had once given themselves over to sensual indulgences. Manius Curius had been intimate with P. Decius, who four years before the former's consulship had devoted himself to death for the Republic. Both Fabricius and Coruncanius knew him also, and from the experience of their own lives, as well as from the action of P. Decius, they were of opinion that there did exist something intrinsically noble and great, which was sought for its own sake, and at which all the best men aimed, to the contempt and neglect of pleasure. Why then do I spend so many words on the subject of pleasure? Why, because, far from being a charge against old age, that it does not much feel the want of any pleasures, it is its highest praise.

But, you will say, it is deprived of the pleasures of the table, the heaped–up board, the rapid passing of the wine–cup. Well, then, it is also free from headache, disordered digestion, broken sleep. But if we must grant pleasure something, since we do not find it easy to resist its charms,—for Plato, with happy inspiration, calls pleasure "vice's bait," because of course men are caught by it as fish by a hook,—yet, although old age has to abstain from extravagant banquets, it is still capable of enjoying modest festivities. As a boy I often used to see Gaius Duilius, the son of Marcus, then an old man, returning from a dinner–party. He thoroughly enjoyed the frequent use of torch and flute–player, distinctions which he had assumed though unprecedented in the case of a private person. It was the privilege of his glory. But why mention others? I will come back to my own case. To begin with, I have always remained a member of a "club"—clubs, you know, were established in my quæstorship on the reception of the Magna Mater from Ida. So I used to dine at their feast with the members of my club—on the whole with moderation, though there was a certain warmth of temperament natural to my time of life; but as that advances there is a daily decrease of all excitement. Nor was I, in fact, ever wont to measure my enjoyment even of these banquets by the physical pleasures they gave more than by the gathering and conversation of friends. For it was a good idea of our ancestors to style the presence of guests at a dinner–table—seeing that it implied a community of enjoyment—a convivium, "a living together." It is a better term than the Greek words which mean "a drinking together" or "an eating together." For they would seem to give the preference to what is really the least important part of it.

For myself, owing to the pleasure I take in conversation, I enjoy even banquets that begin early in the afternoon, and not only in company with my contemporaries—of whom very few survive—but also with men of your age and with yourselves. I am thankful to old age, which has increased my avidity for conversation, while it has removed that for eating and drinking. But if any one does enjoy these—not to seem to have proclaimed war against all pleasure without exception, which is perhaps a feeling inspired by nature—I fail to perceive even in these very pleasures that old age is entirely without the power of appreciation. For myself, I take delight even in the old–fashioned appointment of master of the feast; and in the arrangement of the conversation, which according to ancestral custom is begun from the last place on the left–hand couch when the wine is brought in; as also in the cups which, as in Xenophon's banquet, are small and filled by driblets; and in the contrivance for cooling in summer, and for warming by the winter sun or winter fire. These things I keep up even among my Sabine countrymen, and every day have a full dinner–party of neighbours, which we prolong as far into the night as we can with varied conversation.

But you may urge—there is not the same tingling sensation of pleasure in old men. No doubt; but neither do they miss it so much. For nothing gives you uneasiness which you do not miss. That was a fine answer of Sophocles to a man who asked him, when in extreme old age, whether he was still a lover. "Heaven forbid!" he replied; "I was only too glad to escape from that, as though from a boorish and insane master." To men indeed who are keen after such things it may possibly appear disagreeable and uncomfortable to be without them; but to jaded appetites it is pleasanter to lack than to enjoy. However, he cannot be said to lack who does not want: my contention is that not to want is the pleasanter thing.

But even granting that youth enjoys these pleasures with more zest; in the first place, they are insignificant things to enjoy, as I have said; and in the second place, such as age is not entirely without, if it does not possess them in profusion. Just as a man gets greater pleasure from Ambivius Turpio if seated in the front row at the theatre than if he was in the last, yet, after all, the man in the last row does get pleasure; so youth, because it looks at pleasures at closer quarters, perhaps enjoys itself more, yet even old age, looking at them from a distance, does enjoy itself well enough. Why, what blessings are these—that the soul, having served its time, so to speak, in the campaigns of desire and ambition, rivalry and hatred, and all the passions, should live in its own thoughts, and, as the expression goes, should dwell apart! Indeed, if it has in store any of what I may call the food of study and philosophy, nothing can be pleasanter than an old age of leisure. We were witnesses to C. Gallus—a friend of your father's, Scipio—intent to the day of his death on mapping out the sky and land. How often did the light surprise him while still working out a problem begun during the night! How often did night find him busy on what he had begun at dawn! How he delighted in predicting for us solar and lunar eclipses long before they occurred! Or again in studies of a lighter nature, though still

17

requiring keenness of intellect, what pleasure Nævius took in his Punic War! Plautus in his Truculentus and Pseudolus! I even saw Livius Andronicus, who, having produced a play six years before I was born—in the consulship of Cento and Tuditanus—lived till I had become a young man. Why speak of Publius Licinius Crassus' devotion to pontifical and civil law, or of the Publius Scipio of the present time, who within these last few days has been created Pontifex Maximus? And yet I have seen all whom I have mentioned ardent in these pursuits when old men. Then there is Marcus Cethegus, whom Ennius justly called "Persuasion's Marrow"—with what enthusiasm did we see him exert himself in oratory even when quite old! What pleasures are there is feasts, games, or mistresses comparable to pleasures such as these? And they are all tastes, too, connected with learning, which in men of sense and good education grow with their growth. It is indeed an honourable sentiment which Solon expresses in a verse which I have quoted before—that he grew old learning many a fresh lesson every day. Than that intellectual pleasure none certainly can be greater.

I come now to the pleasures of the farmer, in which I take amazing delight. These are not hindered by any extent of old age, and seem to me to approach nearest to the ideal wise man's life. For he has to deal with the earth, which never refuses its obedience, nor ever returns what it has received without usury; sometimes, indeed, with less, but generally with greater interest. For my part, however, it is not merely the thing produced, but the earth's own force and natural productiveness that delight me. For having received in its bosom the seed scattered broadcast upon it, softened and broken up, she first keeps it concealed therein (hence the harrowing which accomplishes this gets its name from a word meaning "to hide"); next, when it has been warmed by her heat and close pressure, she splits it open and draws from it the greenery of the blade. This, supported by the fibres of the root, little by little grows up, and held upright by its jointed stalk is enclosed in sheaths, as being still immature. When it has emerged from them it produces an ear of corn arranged in order, and is defended against the pecking of the smaller birds by a regular palisade of spikes.

Need I mention the starting, planting, and growth of vines? I can never have too much of this pleasure—to let you into the secret of what gives my old age repose and amusement. For I say nothing here of the natural force which all things propagated from the earth possess—the earth which from that tiny grain in a fig, or the grapestone in a grape, or the most minute seeds of the other cereals and plants, produces such huge trunks and boughs. Mallet—shoots, slips, cuttings, quicksets, layers—are they not enough to fill any one with delight and astonishment? The vine by nature is apt to fall, and unless supported drops down to the earth; yet in order to keep itself upright it embraces whatever it reaches with its tendrils as though they were hands. Then as it creeps on, spreading itself in intricate and wild profusion, the dresser's art prunes it with the knife and prevents it growing a forest of shoots and expanding to excess in every direction. Accordingly at the beginning of spring in the shoots which have been left there protrudes at each of the joints what is termed an "eye." From this the grape emerges and shows itself; which, swollen by the juice of the earth and the heat of the sun, is at first very bitter to the taste, but afterwards grows sweet as it matures; and being covered with tendrils is never without a moderate warmth, and yet is able to ward off the fiery heat of the sun. Can anything be richer in product or more beautiful to contemplate? It is not its utility only, as I said before, that charms me, but the method of its cultivation and the natural process of its growth: the rows of uprights, the cross–pieces for the tops of the plants, the tying up of the vines and their propagation by layers, the pruning, to which I have already referred, of some shoots, the setting of others. I need hardly mention irrigation, or trenching and digging the soil, which much increase its fertility. As to the advantages of manuring I have spoken in my book on agriculture. The learned Hesiod did not say a single word on this subject, though he was writing on the cultivation of the soil; yet Homer, who in my opinion was many generations earlier, represents Lærtes as softening his regret for his son by cultivating and manuring his farm. Nor is it only in cornfields and meadows and vineyards and plantations that a farmer's life is made cheerful. There are the garden and the orchard, the feeding of sheep, the swarms of bees, endless varieties of flowers. Nor is it only planting out that charms: there is also grafting—surely the most ingenious invention ever made by husbandmen.

I might continue my list of the delights of country life; but even what I have said I think is somewhat overlong. However, you must pardon me; for farming is a very favourite hobby of mine, and old age is naturally rather garrulous—for I would not be thought to acquit it of all faults.

Well, it was in a life of this sort that Manius Curius, after celebrating triumphs over the Samnites, the Sabines, and Pyrrhus, spent his last days. When I look at his villa—for it is not far from my own—I never can enough admire the man's own frugality or the spirit of the age. As Curius was sitting at his hearth the Samnites, who brought him a large sum of gold, were repulsed by him; for it was not, he said, a fine thing in his eyes to possess gold, but to rule those who possessed it. Could such a high spirit fail to make old age

On Old Age

pleasant?

But to return to farmers—not to wander from my own mètier. In those days there were senators, i. e., old men, on their farms. For L. Quinctius Cincinnatus was actually at the plough when word was brought him that he had been named Dictator. It was by his order as Dictator, by the way, that C. Servilius Ahala, the Master of the Horse, seized and put to death Spurius Mælius when attempting to obtain royal power. Curius as well as other old men used to receive their summonses to attend the Senate in their farm–houses, from which circumstances the summoners were called viatores or "travellers." Was these men's old age an object of pity who found their pleasure in the cultivation of the land? In my opinion, scarcely any life can be more blessed, not alone from its utility (for agriculture is beneficial to the whole human race), but also as much from the mere pleasure of the thing, to which I have already alluded, and from the rich abundance and supply of all things necessary for the food of man and for the worship of the gods above. So, as these are objects of desire to certain people, let us make our peace with pleasure. For the good and hard–working farmer's wine–cellar and oil–store, as well as his larder, are always well filled, and his whole farm–house is richly furnished. It abounds in pigs, goats, lambs, fowls, milk, cheese, and honey. Then there is the garden, which the farmers themselves call their "second flitch." A zest and flavour is added to all these by hunting and fowling in spare hours. Need I mention the greenery of meadows, the rows of trees, the beauty of vineyard and olive–grove? I will put it briefly: nothing can either furnish necessaries more richly, or present a fairer spectacle, than well–cultivated land. And to the enjoyment of that, old age does not merely present no hindrance—it actually invites and allures to it. For where else can it better warm itself, either by basking in the sun or by sitting by the fire, or at the proper time cool itself more wholesomely by the help of shade or water? Let the young keep their arms then to themselves, their horses, spears, their foils and ball, their swimming–baths and running–path. To us old men let them, out of the many forms of sport, leave dice and counters; but even that as they choose, since old age can be quite happy without them.

Xenophon's books are very useful for many purposes. Pray go on reading them with attention, as you have ever done. In what ample terms is agriculture lauded by him in the book about husbanding one's property, which is called Oeconomicus! But to show you that he thought nothing so worthy of a prince as the taste for cultivating the soil, I will translate what Socrates says to Critobulus in that book:

On Old Age

"When that most gallant Lacedæmonian, Lysander, came to visit the Persian prince Cyrus at Sardis, so eminent for his character and the glory of his rule, bringing him presents from his allies, he treated Lysander in all ways with courteous familiarity and kindness, and, among other things, took him to see a certain park carefully planted. Lysander expressed admiration of the height of the trees and the exact arrangement of their rows in the quincunx, the careful cultivation of the soil, its freedom from weeds, and the sweetness of the odours exhaled from the flowers, and went on to say that what he admired was not the industry only, but also the skill of the man by whom this had been planned and laid out. Cyrus replied: 'Well, it was I who planned the whole thing; these rows are my doing, the laying out is all mine: many of the trees were even planted by my own hand.' Then Lysander, looking at his purple robe, the brilliance of his person, and his adornment Persian fashion with gold and many jewels, said: 'People are quite right, Cyrus, to call you happy, since the advantages of high fortune have been joined to an excellence like yours.'"

This kind of good fortune, then, it is in the power of old men to enjoy; nor is age any bar to our maintaining pursuits of every other kind, and especially of agriculture, to the very extreme verge of old age. For instance, we have it on record that M. Valerius Corvus kept it up to his hundredth year, living on his land and cultivating it after his active career was over, though between his first and sixth consulships there was an interval of six and forty years. So that he had an official career lasting the number of years which our ancestors defined as coming between birth and the beginning of old age. Moreover, that last period of his old age was more blessed than that of his middle life, inasmuch as he had greater influence and less labour. For the crowning grace of old age is influence.

How great was that of L. Cæcilius Metellus! How great that of Atilius Calatinus, over whom the famous epitaph was placed, "Very many classes agree in deeming this to have been the very first man of the nation"! The line cut on his tomb is well known. It is natural, then, that a man should have had influence, in whose praise the verdict of history is unanimous. Again, in recent times, what a great man was Publius Crassus, Pontifex Maximus, and his successor in the same office, M. Lepidus! I need scarcely mention Paulus or Africanus, or, as I did before, Maximus. It was not only their senatorial utterances that had weight: their least gesture had it also. In fact, old age, especially when it has enjoyed honours, has an influence worth all the pleasures of youth put together.

On Old Age

But throughout my discourse remember that my panegyric applies to an old age that has been established on foundations laid by youth. From which may be deduced what I once said with universal applause, that it was a wretched old age that had to defend itself by speech. Neither white hairs nor wrinkles can at once claim influence in themselves: it is the honourable conduct of earlier days that is rewarded by possessing influence at the last. Even things generally regarded as trifling and matters of course—being saluted, being courted, having way made for one, people rising when one approaches, being escorted to and from the forum, being referred to for advice—all these are marks of respect, observed among us and in other States—always most sedulously where the moral tone is highest. They say that Lysander the Spartan, whom I have mentioned before, used to remark that Sparta was the most dignified home for old age; for that nowhere was more respect paid to years, nowhere was old age held in higher honour. Nay, the story is told of how when a man of advanced years came into the theatre at Athens when the games were going on, no place was given him anywhere in that large assembly by his own countrymen; but when he came near the Lacedæmonians, who as ambassadors had a fixed place assigned to them, they rose as one man out of respect for him, and gave the veteran a seat. When they were greeted with rounds of applause from the whole audience, one of them remarked: "The Athenians know what is right, but will not do it."

There are many excellent rules in our augural college, but among the best is one which affects our subject—that precedence in speech goes by seniority; and augurs who are older are preferred not only to those who have held higher office, but even to those who are actually in possession of imperium. What then are the physical pleasures to be compared with the reward of influence? Those who have employed it with distinction appear to me to have played the drama of life to its end, and not to have broken down in the last act like unpractised players.

But, it will be said, old men are fretful, fidgety, ill–tempered, and disagreeable. If you come to that, they are also avaricious. But these are faults of character, not of the time of life. And, after all, fretfulness and the other faults I mentioned admit of some excuse—not, indeed, a complete one, but one that may possibly pass muster: they think themselves neglected, looked down upon, mocked. Besides, with bodily weakness every rub is a source of pain. Yet all these faults are softened both by good character and good education. Illustrations of this may be found in real life, as also on the stage in the case of the brothers in the Adelphi. What harshness in the one, what gracious manners in the other! The fact is that, just as it is not every wine, so it is not every life, that turns sour from keeping. Serious gravity I approve of in old age, but, as in other things, it must be within due limits: bitterness I can in no case approve. What the object of senile avarice may be I cannot conceive. For can there be anything more absurd than to seek more journey money, the less there remains of the journey?

There remains the fourth reason, which more than anything else appears to torment men of my age and keep them in a flutter—THE NEARNESS OF DEATH, which, it must be allowed, cannot be far from an old man. But what a poor dotard must he be who has not learnt in the course of so long a life that death is not a thing to be feared? Death, that is either to be totally disregarded, if it entirely extinguishes the soul, or is even to be desired, if it brings him where he is to exist forever. A third alternative, at any rate, cannot possibly be discovered. Why then should I be afraid if I am destined either not to be miserable after death or even to be happy? After all, who is such a fool as to feel certain—however young he may be—that he will be alive in the evening? Nay, that time of life has many more chances of death than ours. Young men more easily contract diseases; their illnesses are more serious; their treatment has to be more severe. Accordingly, only a few arrive at old age. If that were not so, life would be conducted better and more wisely; for it is in old men that thought, reason, and prudence are to be found; and if there had been no old men, States would never have existed at all. But I return to the subject of the imminence of death. What sort of charge is this against old age, when you see that it is shared by youth? I had reason in the case of my excellent son—as you had, Scipio, in that of your brothers, who were expected to attain the highest honours—to realise that death is common to every time of life. Yes, you will say; but a young man expects to live long; an old man cannot expect to do so. Well, he is a fool to expect it. For what can be more foolish than to regard the uncertain as certain, the false as true? "An old man has nothing even to hope." Ah, but it is just there that he is in a better position than a young man, since what the latter only hopes he has obtained. The one wishes to live long; the other has lived long.

And yet, good heavens! what is "long" in a man's life? For grant the utmost limit: let us expect an age like that of the King of the Tartessi. For there was, as I find recorded, a certain Agathonius at Gades who reigned eighty years and lived a hundred and twenty. But to my mind nothing seems even long in which there is any "last," for when that arrives, then all the past has slipped away—only that remains to which you have attained by virtue and righteous actions. Hours indeed, and days and months and years depart, nor does past time ever return, nor can the future be known. Whatever time each is granted

23

for life, with that he is bound to be content. An actor, in order to earn approval, is not bound to perform the play from beginning to end; let him only satisfy the audience in whatever act he appears. Nor need a wise man go on to the concluding "plaudite." For a short term of life is long enough for living well and honourably. But if you go farther, you have no more right to grumble than farmers do because the charm of the spring season is past and the summer and autumn have come. For the word "spring" in a way suggests youth, and points to the harvest to be: the other seasons are suited for the reaping and storing of the crops. Now the harvest of old age is, as I have often said, the memory and rich store of blessings laid up in earlier life. Again, all things that accord with nature are to be counted as good. But what can be more in accordance with Nature than for old men to die? A thing, indeed, which also befalls young men, though Nature revolts and fights against it. Accordingly, the death of young men seems to me like putting out a great fire with a deluge of water; but old men die like a fire going out because it has burnt down of its own nature without artificial means. Again, just as apples when unripe are torn from trees, but when ripe and mellow drop down, so it is violence that takes life from young men, ripeness from old. This ripeness is so delightful to me that, as I approach nearer to death, I seem, as it were, to be sighting land, and to be coming to port at last after a long voyage.

Again, there is no fixed border–line for old age, and you are making a good and proper use of it as long as you can satisfy the call of duty and disregard death. The result of this is, that old age is even more confident and courageous than youth. That is the meaning of Solon's answer to the tyrant Pisistratus. When the latter asked him what he relied upon in opposing him with such boldness, he is said to have replied, "On my old age." But that end of life is the best when, without the intellect or senses being impaired, Nature herself takes to pieces her own handiwork which she also put together. Just as the builder of a ship or a house can break them up more easily than any one else, so the Nature that knit together the human frame can also best unfasten it. Moreover, a thing freshly glued together is always difficult to pull asunder; if old, this is easily done.

The result is that the short time of life left to them is not to be grasped at by old men with greedy eagerness, or abandoned without cause. Pythagoras forbids us, without an order from our commander, that is God, to desert life's fortress and outpost. Solon's epitaph, indeed, is that of a wise man, in which he says that he does not wish his death to be unaccompanied by the sorrow and lamentations of his friends. He wants, I suppose, to be beloved by them. But I rather think Ennius says better:

On Old Age

None grace me with their tears, nor weeping loud

Make sad my funeral rites!

He holds that a death is not a subject for mourning when it is followed by immortality.

Again, there may possibly be some sensation of dying—and that only for a short time, especially in the case of an old man: after death, indeed, sensation is either what one would desire, or it disappears altogether. But to disregard death is a lesson which must be studied from our youth up; for unless that is learnt, no one can have a quiet mind. For die we certainly must, and that too without being certain whether it may not be this very day. A death, therefore, is hanging over our head every hour, how can a man ever be unshaken in soul if he fears it?

But on this theme I don't think I need much enlarge: when I remember what Lucius Brutus did, who was killed while defending his country; or the two Decii, who spurred their horses to a gallop and met a voluntary death; or M. Atilius Regulus, who left his home to confront a death of torture, rather than break the word which he had pledged to the enemy; or the two Scipios, who determined to block the Carthaginian advance even with their own bodies; or your grandfather Lucius Paulus, who paid with his life for the rashness of his colleague in the disgrace at Cannæ; or M. Marcellus, whose death not even the most bloodthirsty of enemies would allow to go without the honour of burial. It is enough to recall that our legions (as I have recorded in my Origins) have often marched with cheerful and lofty spirit to ground from which they believed that they would never return. That, therefore, which young men—not only uninstructed, but absolutely ignorant—treat as of no account, shall men who are neither young nor ignorant shrink from in terror? As a general truth, as it seems to me, it is weariness of all pursuits that creates weariness of life. There are certain pursuits adapted to childhood: do young men miss them? There are others suited to early manhood: does that settled time of life called "middle age" ask for them? There are others, again, suited to that age, but not looked for in old age. There are, finally, some which belong to old age. Therefore, as the pursuits of the earlier ages have their time for disappearing, so also have those of old age. And when that takes place, a satiety of life brings on the ripe time for death.

For I do not see why I should not venture to tell you my personal opinion as to death, of which I seem to myself to have a clearer vision in proportion as I am nearer to it. I believe, Scipio and Lælius, that your fathers—those illustrious men and my dearest friends—are still alive, and that too with a life which alone deserves the name. For as long as we are imprisoned in this framework of the body, we perform a certain function and laborious work assigned us by fate. The soul, in fact, is of heavenly origin, forced down from its home in the highest, and, so to speak, buried in earth, a place quite opposed to its divine nature and its immortality. But I suppose the immortal gods to have sown souls broadcast in human bodies, that there might be some to survey the world, and while contemplating the order of the heavenly bodies to imitate it in the unvarying regularity of their life. Nor is it only reason and arguments that have brought me to this belief, but the great fame and authority of the most distinguished philosophers. I used to be told that Pythagoras and the Pythagoreans—almost natives of our country, who in old times had been called the Italian school of philosophers—never doubted that we had souls drafted from the universal Divine intelligence. I used besides to have pointed out to me the discourse delivered by Socrates on the last day of his life upon the immortality of the soul—Socrates, who was pronounced by the oracle at Delphi to be the wisest of men. I need say no more. I have convinced myself, and I hold—in view of the rapid movement of the soul, its vivid memory of the past and its prophetic knowledge of the future, its many accomplishments, its vast range of knowledge, its numerous discoveries—that a nature embracing such varied gifts cannot itself be mortal. And since the soul is always in motion and yet has no external source of motion, for it is self–moved, I conclude that it will also have no end to its motion, because it is not likely ever to abandon itself. Again, since the nature of the soul is not composite, nor has in it any admixture that is not homogeneous and similar, I conclude that it is indivisible, and, if indivisible, that it cannot perish. It is again a strong proof of men knowing most things before birth, that when mere children they grasp innumerable facts with such speed as to show that they are not then taking them in for the first time, but remembering and recalling them. This is roughly Plato's argument.

Once more in Xenophon we have the elder Cyrus on his deathbed speaking as follows:—

"Do not suppose, my dearest sons, that when I have left you I shall be nowhere and no one. Even when I was with you, you did not see my soul, but knew that it was in this body of mine from what I did. Believe then that it is still the same, even though you see it not. The honours paid to illustrious men had not continued to exist after their death, had the souls of these very men not done something to make us retain our recollection of them beyond the ordinary time. For myself, I never could be persuaded that soul while in mortal bodies were alive, and died directly they left them; nor, in fact, that the soul only lost all intelligence when it left the unintelligent body. I believe rather that when, by being liberated from all corporeal admixture, it has begun to be pure and undefiled, it is then that it becomes wise. And again, when man's natural frame is resolved into its elements by death, it is clearly seen whither each of the other elements departs: for they all go to the place from which they came: but the soul alone is invisible alike when present and when departing. Once more, you see that nothing is so like death as sleep. And yet it is in sleepers that souls most clearly reveal their divine nature; for they foresee many events when they are allowed to escape and are left free. This shows what they are likely to be when they have completely freed themselves from the fetters of the body. Wherefore, if these things are so, obey me as a god. But if my soul is to perish with my body, nevertheless do you from awe of the gods, who guard and govern this fair universe, preserve my memory by the loyalty and piety of your lives."

Such are the words of the dying Cyrus. I will now, with your good leave, look at home. No one, my dear Scipio, shall ever persuade me that your father, Paulus, and your two grandfathers, Paulus and Africanus, or the father of Africanus, or his uncle, or many other illustrious men not necessary to mention, would have attempted such lofty deeds as to be remembered by posterity, had they not seen in their minds that future ages concerned them. Do you suppose—to take an old man's privilege of a little self–praise—that I should have been likely to undertake such heavy labours by day and night, at home and abroad, if I had been destined to have the same limit to my glory as to my life? Had it not been much better to pass an age of ease and repose without any labour or exertion? But my soul, I know not how, refusing to be kept down, ever fixed its eyes upon future ages, as though from a conviction that it would begin to live only when it had left the body. But had it not been the case that souls were immortal, it would not have been the souls of all the best men that made the greatest efforts after an immortality of fame.

Again, is there not the fact that the wisest man ever dies with the greatest cheerfulness, the most unwise with the least? Don't you think that the soul which has the clearer and longer sight sees that it is starting for better things, while the soul whose vision is dimmer does not see it? For my part, I am transported with the desire to see your fathers, who were the object of my reverence and affection. Nor is it only those whom I knew that I long to see; it is those also of whom I have been told and have read, whom I have myself recorded in my history. When I am setting out for that, there is certainly no one who will find it easy to draw me back, or boil me up again like second Pelios. Nay, if some god should grant me to renew my childhood from my present age and once more to be crying in my cradle, I would firmly refuse; nor should I in truth be willing, after having, as it were, run the full course, to be recalled from the winning–crease to the barriers. For what blessing has life to offer? Should we not rather say, what labour? But granting that it has, at any rate it has after all a limit either to enjoyment or to existence. I don't wish to depreciate life, as many men and good philosophers have often done; nor do I regret having lived, for I have done so in a way that lets me think that I was not born in vain. But I quit life as I would an inn, not as I would a home. For nature has given us a place of entertainment, not of residence.

Oh, glorious day when I shall set out to join that heavenly conclave and company of souls, and depart from the turmoil and impurities of this world! For I shall not go to join only those whom I have before mentioned, but also my son Cato, than whom no better man was ever born, nor one more conspicuous for piety. His body was burnt by me, though mine ought, on the contrary, to have been burnt by him; but his spirit, not abandoning, but ever looking back upon me, has certainly gone whither he saw that I too must come. I was thought to bear that loss heroically, not that I really bore it without distress, but I found my own consolation in the thought that the parting and separation between us was not to be for long.

It is by these means, my dear Scipio,—for you said that you and Lælius were wont to express surprise on this point,—that my old age sits lightly on me, and is not only not oppressive but even delightful. But if I am wrong in thinking the human soul immortal, I am glad to be wrong; nor will I allow the mistake which gives me so much pleasure to be wrested from me as long as I live. But if when dead, as some insignificant philosophers think, I am to be without sensation, I am not afraid of dead philosophers deriding my errors. Again, if we are not to be immortal, it is nevertheless what a man must wish—to have his life end at its proper time. For nature puts a limit to living as to everything else. Now, old age is, as it were, the playing out of the drama, the full fatigue of which we should shun, especially when we also feel that we have had more than enough of it.

This is all I had to say on old age. I pray that you may arrive at it, that you may put my words to a practical test.

LaVergne, TN USA
13 February 2011
216400LV00004B/177/A